# PALEO FAST FOOD

## 26 Super Quick And Make-Ahead Recipes For When You're On The Go

### (Primal Gluten Free Cookbook)

Kate Evans Scott

This book is dedicated to my two beautiful children.

# ACKNOWLEDGMENTS

Thank You to my friends and family for your encouragement. Your support has been the cornerstone of this creative process.

A special thanks also goes out to you the reader ~ I am grateful to be sharing this journey to health and happiness together with you.

# CONTENTS

# PALEO MADE FAST AND SIMPLE

Preparing a Paleo meal is quite different now from the time of our caveman ancestors. We don't have to hunt down the meat with a spear, or spend all day foraging for berries and cracking nuts. However, compared to our modern day prepackaged convenience foods, prepping a Paleo meal can often seem exhausting.

There are very few prepared foods that meet the Paleo Diet guidelines - free of refined sugars, grains, and dairy as well as chemicals used in processing. Aside from hitting the salad bar at your local health food market, there aren't too many options for dining on the fly.

But don't fret, and don't quit. With a little bit of forethought and preparation, you can stock your fridge and pantry to make mealtime less stressful and still eat a healthy, filling diet.

# STOCK YOUR PANTRY

While eating fresh and organic meats and produce is always the first choice, our modern lifestyles don't always allow us time to bake the pumpkin or home-can tomatoes.  Here are some pantry staples that will last a long time in your cupboard, and can be opened and used when needed.  Make sure you are choosing brands that are organic (whenever possible) and free of hidden sugars and processing chemicals.

- Canned pumpkin puree
- Chicken, beef, and vegetable broth
- Canned diced tomatoes
- Tomato sauce
- Nuts and seeds (all kinds)
- Canned coconut milk
- Coconut oil, olive oil, nut oils, sesame seed oil
- Dried fruits
- Shredded coconut
- Grain-free LARA™ bars (for snacking)
- Almond and other nut butter
- Raw honey
- Pure maple syrup
- Dried spices and sea salt
- Onions and sweet potatoes
- Unsweetened applesauce
- Paleo People™ Granola (or make your own)
- Nick's Sticks™ Grass-Fed Beef sticks or homemade jerky (for quick protein)

# STOCK YOUR REFRIGERATOR

As a Paleo eater, the bulk of your food is going to be fresh fruits and vegetables, which will be stored primarily in the refrigerator. There are also a few handy condiments, sauces, and prepared foods to keep chilled in the icebox for convenient cooking.

- Prepared guacamole (make sure to read the label)
- Organic apple butter, like Knudsen's Organic
- Prepared fresh salsa (check the label for added sugar)
- Cubed butternut squash from the grocery cooler
- Gluten free Worcestershire sauce
- Prepared chopped vegetables
- Pre-washed baby greens (spinach, kale, field greens)
- Meats of all kinds (best form a local farm)
- Fully cooked smoked sausage (best from a local farm)
- Deli mustard, all varieties (garlic, spicy, etc)
- Eggs - always have eggs!
- Julian Bakery™ Paleo Breads and wraps
- Liquid coconut aminos
- Almond milk

# STOCK YOUR FREEZER

If you have an extra deep freezer, you're in a really good position to stock up on farm-raised meats and home-frozen fruits and veggies - picked, blanched, and frozen when they're in season. If you don't have an extra freezer, don't worry. You can still stock up on some staples and even have room to throw a few pre-made meals in there, too.

While it's always best to eat fresh, frozen fruits and vegetables are picked at the height of ripeness and quick-frozen to preserve the most vitamins and nutrients possible. They are actually a better choice than out-of-season produce that has been shipped from all ends of the earth. Pre-cut frozen veggies can cut dinner-prep time in half, and some frozen fruit makes a breakfast smoothie a snap. Stack your freezer for the week and see how easy it is to stay on track.

- Frozen diced onion
- Frozen pepper and onion blend
- Frozen broccoli and/or cauliflower
- Frozen greens (cut-leaf spinach, collards, kale)
- Frozen okra
- Frozen stir-fry and/or soup veggie blends
- Frozen fruits (pineapple, mango, strawberries, blueberries, blackberries, pomegranate arills, raspberries, peaches, etc.)
- Meats: Buy when they're on sale, or purchase a whole, half, or quarter of an animal (cows and pigs, generally) from a local farm. Make sure the meats are completely sealed tight so you don't end up with freezer burn.
- Whole roaster chickens and chicken pieces from your local farmer (farmer's market) or health food store.
- Broth (made from previously roasted chickens and meats)
- Julian Bakery™ Paleo Breads (or other brand)

The following recipes are simple recipes that can either be pre-made for later use, prepped in the morning and slow-cooked for supper, or are just really quick and easy. Use the Quick Reference Guide on the next page to help you find a recipe that works in your busy day, and see how sticking to your Paleo menu is made fast and simple.

# PALEO FAST FOOD

## QUICK REFERENCE GUIDE:

 **PANTRY STAPLE**

 **QUICK**

 **PRE-WORKOUT**

 **POST-WORKOUT**

# PALEO
## FAST FOOD

## QUICK REFERENCE GUIDE:

 **TAKE AWAY**

 **FREEZER**

 **SLOW COOKER**

# BREAKFAST

Breakfast is the most important meal of the day. It jump-starts the metabolism and gives you the fuel you need for chasing down mammoths... or just getting the kids to school on time! By stocking your pantry and fridge with the right stuff, you'll have breakfast in hand and be out the door with time to spare!

# BREAKFAST MENU

ESSENTIAL GRANOLA (PANTRY STAPLE)

SLOW COOKER COCONUT YOGURT (SLOW-COOKER)

CHORIZO AND EGGS (QUICK)

BERRY BREAKFAST SMOOTHIE (QUICK)

SAUSAGE N' SQUASH SKILLET (QUICK)

PALEO FRENCH TOAST (QUICK / FREEZER)

SWEET POTATO HASH N' EGGS (QUICK / POST-WORKOUT)

BANANA BREAD GREEN SMOOTHIE (QUICK / PRE-WORKOUT)

HAZELNUT WAFFLES (QUICK / FREEZER)

ESSENTIAL
GRANOLA

# ESSENTIAL GRANOLA

This hearty, crunchy, slightly sweet granola is perfect for topping coconut yogurt or for eating as a cereal with almond milk and sliced banana. Make a big batch at the start of the week and store it in mason jars or airtight containers in the pantry for up to two weeks.

**Essential Granola Recipe:**

**Ingredients:**
- 1 cup raw almonds
- ½ cup chopped hazelnuts
- 1 cup shredded, unsweetened coconut
- 1 – 2 Tbsp pure maple syrup
- 1 heaping Tbsp coconut oil, softened
- 1 tsp ground cinnamon
- ½ cup raisins

**Directions:** Place all ingredients, except raisins, into your food processor. Pulse a few times to chop the nuts and coconut into lentil-sized pieces. These should not be ground down really fine. You want to see chunks.

Spread the mixture onto a parchment-lined jelly roll pan. Turn on the oven to 200°F and place the pan on the center rack. Bake for about an hour, and then turn over the mixture with a spatula. Allow to cook another hour or more until the granola is crisp, but not burned.

Remove from oven and allow to cool, then mix in the raisins. Store in an airtight container for up to two weeks.

Serving Size: ½ cup          Yields: 6 servings
Prep Time: 5 min             Bake Time: 2 hours
Total Time: 2 hrs, 5 min

COCONUT
YOGURT

# SLOW COOKER COCONUT YOGURT

If you're a yogurt fan, this recipe will bring you back to the breakfast table! Coconut milk is the base, and any powdered probiotic provides the bacteria necessary to culture the milk into yogurt. Make sure you don't skip the maple syrup, though. That bacteria needs something to "eat!" I make this each Sunday, because we're usually home and able to easily turn the pot on and off. This way, we start out Monday with a batch of yogurt to last the week! I like to store it in individual cups with fruit on top for breakfast or lunch on the run.

**Coconut Yogurt Recipe:**

**Ingredients:**
- 3 15-0z cans full-fat coconut milk
- 2 Tbsp pure maple syrup
- ½ tsp powdered probiotic of choice
- 1 Tbsp tapioca starch (optional- for thickening)

**Directions:** Pour the coconut milk into a slow cooker set on high. Heat for 2 ½ hours, then turn off the slow cooker and allow the milk to come down to room temperature (about 110°F on a candy thermometer). Just walk away and do something else during this time.

Whisk the maple syrup, probiotic of choice, and tapioca starch (if using) into the warm milk. Wrap the entire crock-pot in two layers of thick towel. This helps maintain the temperature. Let it sit overnight. DO NOT open the towels or crock-pot during this time.

In the morning, you have coconut yogurt. If you did not use thickener, the yogurt may be thin. You can thicken it by blending in your favorite fruits in the blender, or by whisking in a little bit of tapioca starch. The yogurt will thicken as it cools.

Pour the yogurt into individual glass jars (topped with fruit, like the blackberries shown here) or into one large airtight container. Store in the refrigerator up to ten days (if you don't gobble it up first).

Serving Size: ½ cup     Yields: 6 servings
Prep Time: 5 min     Slow-Cooker Time: 2 ½ hrs + overnight

CHORIZO
AND EGGS

# CHORIZO AND EGGS

Chorizo is a spicy Mexican sausage that comes fully cooked and pairs well with fluffy scrambled egg. For a hearty full breakfast, serve the chorizo and eggs with sweet potato hash browns. The sweet and spicy are a perfect combo.

**Chorizo And Eggs Recipe:**

**Ingredients:**
- 6 eggs
- ½ cup pre-diced onion (fresh or frozen)
- 1 link chorizo sausage
- 1 Tbsp grass-fed butter or coconut oil
- 1 Tbsp water

**Directions:**  Heat the butter or coconut oil in a large pan over medium heat. Beat the eggs with the water until they are slightly frothy and have an even consistency.

Dice the sausage into small pieces.  Place the sausage and onion in the pan and cook for a couple of minutes until the onion is starting to soften.  Add the beaten eggs and cook, turning often with a rubber spatula, until eggs are cooked through.

Serve with a side of sweet potato hash browns or rolled up in a Paleo wrap.

Serving Size:  about ¾ cup          Yields:  4 servings
Prep Time:  5 min          Cook Time:  5 min          Total Time:  10 min

BERRY BREAKFAST
SMOOTHIE

# BERRY BREAKFAST SMOOTHIE

Nothing is quicker on a rushed morning, nor more satisfying to a hungry tummy, than a nutrient-packed smoothie! This one is filled with dark berries for an antioxidant punch. To add even more protein, substitute almond milk for the cider or juice.

**Berry Breakfast Smoothie Recipe:**

**Ingredients:**
- 1 cup fresh or frozen blackberries
- 1 cup fresh or frozen blueberries
- 1 cup packed baby spinach
- 1 banana
- 2 tsp chia seeds
- ½ cup apple cider or fresh apple juice

**Directions:** Peel the banana and place all ingredients into your high-powered blender. Process on low until it moves easily, then turn it up to high and process until smooth. Pour into a tall glass (or travel cup) and enjoy!

Serving Size: About 2 ½ cups          Yields: 1 serving
Prep Time: 2 min          Blend Time: 3 min          Total Time: 5 min

SAUSAGE N'
SQUASH SKILLET

# SAUSAGE N' SQUASH SKILLET

Pre-cubed butternut squash makes this simple one-pot skillet dish a snap. A little grass-fed butter and maple syrup combined with the squash is a perfect complement to savory fresh pork sausage. If you're in a really big hurry, you can slice the sausage and cook it all at once with the squash.

**Sausage N' Squash Skillet Recipe:**

**Ingredients:**
- 6 fresh pork breakfast sausages
- 2 cups cubed butternut squash (fresh, prepackaged)
- 3 tbsp grass-fed butter
- 1 tsp coconut oil
- 1 tbsp pure maple syrup
- Dash cinnamon and nutmeg
- Salt to taste

**Directions:** In a large, heavy skillet, heat the coconut oil over medium heat. Add the sausages and cook until the skin is browned and crisp, and the center is heated through, about 5 minutes. Remove to a plate.

To the same skillet, add the butter and let it melt. Add the squash, maple syrup, and nutmeg. Stir to coat. Cover and cook five minutes. Turn over with a spatula, replace lid, and cook another three minutes. Remove lid and allow the squash to caramelize, about two minutes.

Remove the squash to a plate and top with the sausage. If you are in a bigger hurry, slice the sausage into 1" pieces and cook everything together at the same time by following the cooking instructions for the squash.

Serving Size: 1 cup squash and 3 sausages    Yields: 2 servings
Prep Time: 0    Cook Time: 15 min    Total: 15 min

FRENCH
TOAST

# PALEO FRENCH TOAST

This French toast tastes just like the whole wheat French toast that you remember... only better! When you have Paleo bread on hand, it comes together in a snap, and here's the cool thing, especially if you share your abode with children: Slice the cooked French toast into three strips and freeze in an airtight container. Voila! Paleo French Toast Sticks!

## Paleo French Toast Recipe:

**Ingredients:**
- 2 slices Julian Bakery Paleo Almond or Coconut Bread
- 1 large egg, beaten with 1 tbsp water
- 1 tbsp ghee, grass-fed butter, or coconut oil
- ½ tsp vanilla (optional)
- Pure maple syrup and sliced banana for serving

**Directions:** Beat the egg, water, and vanilla in a shallow bowl until frothy. Heat the butter in a griddle set over medium heat.

Dunk the bread slices in the egg mixture to completely coat. Lay the coated bread on the heated griddle. Cook until golden brown, about two minutes. Flip and cook the other side.

Remove to a plate and top with pure maple syrup and banana slices. Serve with a side of bacon (optional). OR, slice into thirds and freeze for French toast sticks. Reheat in your toaster oven on the dark toast setting.

Serving Size: 2 slices     Yields: 1 serving
Prep Time: 3 min     Cook Time: 4 min     Total Time: 7 min

SWEET POTATO
HASH N' EGGS

# SWEET POTATO HASH N' EGGS

This hash is hearty and quick, and it packs a carbohydrate-protein punch that's perfect for post-workout replenishing. Have an energy bar a half hour before you run that half-marathon in the wee hours of the morning, then whip up this hash for a filling breakfast afterward. You can use orange sweet potatoes for this recipe, but the white sweet potatoes have a milder flavor and won't overpower the rest of the dish.

**Sweet Potato Hash N' Eggs Recipe:**

**Ingredients:**
- 1 large white sweet potato (or traditional sweet potato)
- ½ cup frozen diced white onion
- 1 cup packed baby spinach
- 1 large eggs
- 2 tbsp coconut oil
- 1 tbsp ghee or grass-fed butter
- Salt and black pepper to taste

**Directions:** Roughly peel the sweet potato. Shred in your food processor with the shredding attachment. In a large skillet, heat the coconut oil over medium-high heat. Place the shredded potato and onion in the pan and season with salt and pepper.

While that cooks, heat the ghee in a small pan set over medium heat. Crack the eggs into the pan and cook until the whites are set, but the yolk is still soft, about two minutes. Remove from heat.

Turn the potatoes and cook on the other side until cooked through and crisp. Add the spinach and turn to heat through.

Spoon the hash onto two plates and top with one egg each. Serve with a side of bacon (optional).

Serving Size: ½ recipe with one egg    Yields: 2 servings
Prep Time: 5 min          Cook Time: 10 min          Total Time: 15 min

# BANANA BREAD
# GREEN SMOOTHIE

# BANANA BREAD GREEN SMOOTHIE

Green smoothies are the perfect way to pack a lot of nutrients into one small glass for a super-fast, super-healthy breakfast alternative. This one may look like a glass full of algae, but you'll be surprised at the flavor, which hints at the cinnamon baked goodness of fresh-from-the-oven banana bread!

**Banana Bread Green Smoothie Recipe:**

**Ingredients:**
- 1 cup packed baby spinach or kale
- 1 cup coconut milk or almond milk
- 1 large or two small bananas
- 6 pecan halves
- 3 ice cubes
- 1 tsp pure maple syrup
- ½ tsp vanilla
- ½ tsp cinnamon

**Directions:** Place all ingredients into your high-powered blender and process for two minutes, or until smooth. Pour into a large glass and enjoy!

Serving Size: 2 ½ cups    Yields: 1 serving
Prep Time: 2 min    Blend Time: 2 min    Total Time: 4 min

HAZELNUT
WAFFLES

# HAZELNUT WAFFLES

The waffle iron is a handy kitchen appliance for quick meals, and these waffles are reason enough to have a waffle iron on your kitchen counter. Make a whole batch and freeze what you don't use. They are reheated really well in a toaster oven for breakfast on the go. Top with pure maple syrup, fruit, or even savory toppings.

**Hazelnut Waffle Recipe:**

**Ingredients:**
- 1 cup hazelnut meal
- 3 tbsp coconut flour
- 4 eggs
- ½ cup almond milk
- 2 tbsp melted butter, ghee, or coconut oil
- 1 tbsp raw honey, melted
- 1 tsp cinnamon
- 1 tsp baking powder
- Oil for waffle maker

**Directions:** Preheat your electric waffle iron.
In a medium bowl, whisk together the eggs, milk, butter and honey. In a separate bowl, mix the hazelnut meal, coconut flour, cinnamon, and baking powder.

Slowly stir the liquids into the flour mixture until the batter is consistent and smooth. It will be very thick, not runny like traditional pancake and waffle batter.

If your waffle iron isn't nonstick, coat it with a light brushing of melted coconut oil. Scoop batter into the center of the each waffle spot in the maker, about ¼ cup for each waffle. Close the lid and let cook according to your waffle maker's instructions.

Remove the waffle when it's crispy on the outside, fluffy, and done in the center. Serve with pure maple syrup, fruit, or even topped with a fried egg and sausage! Freeze the remaining waffles in an airtight container and reheat in the toaster oven on a regular toast setting.

Serving Size: 1 waffle      Yields: 4 servings
Prep Time: 5 min      Cook Time: 3 min      Total Time: 8 min

# LUNCHTIME SANDWICHES

Never fear, the sandwich is back to stay. Good old sandwiches might be something you've been missing since starting on the Paleo diet. While there are quite a few good Paleo bread recipes out there, let's face it, baking bread is time consuming. By keeping a few different delicious Paleo breads and wraps from Julian Bakery on hand, you can fall in love with sandwiches all over again! Order the bread online, or go to their web site (www.julianbakery.com) to find a retail location close to you.

# LUNCH SANDWICH MENU

**SPICY TURKEY SANDWICH** (QUICK / TAKE AWAY)
**BACON-APPLE CHICKEN SANDWICH** (QUICK / TAKE AWAY)
**SIMPLE BANANA SANDWICH** (QUICK / TAKE AWAY / PRE-WORKOUT)
**ROAST BEEF AND ARUGULA SANDWICH** (QUICK / TAKE AWAY)
**NAKED TUNA WRAP** (QUICK / TAKE AWAY)

SPICY TURKEY
SANDWICH

# SPICY TURKEY SANDWICH

With Julian Bakery's Coconut Paleo Bread sitting in the fridge, this sandwich comes together in a snap. It's so delicious that you can even make this for your non-Paleo friends and they will absolutely love it! The creaminess of the guacamole is the perfect replacement for mayonnaise, and much healthier. Just remember to check the labels for the guacamole and salsa to make sure there's no added sugar or unacceptable ingredients.

**Spicy Turkey Sandwich Recipe:**

**Ingredients:**
- 2 slices Julian Bakery Coconut Paleo Bread
- 2 oz organic sliced roasted turkey
- 3 Tbsp prepared guacamole
- 2 tsp prepared fresh, spicy salsa (from the grocery cooler)
- 1 leaf Romaine lettuce

**Directions:** Toast the bread in the toaster until just browned and crisp. (Skip this step if you are packing the sandwich in a lunch box for later.) Spread 1 ½ tablespoons of guacamole on one side of each slice of toast. Stack on the turkey and top it with the salsa and lettuce (rinsed and dried). Slice in half and serve with sweet potato chips or a fruit cup.

Serving Size: 1 sandwich      Yields: 1 serving
Prep Time: 5 min      Total Time: 5 min

BACON-APPLE
CHICKEN SANDWICH

# BACON-APPLE CHICKEN SANDWICH

When you're eating a Paleo diet, you have to think outside the box as far as condiments and spreads go... unless you have time to make your own. Knudson Organic Apple Butter gives the perfect sweet-tartness to the salty bacon and roasted deli chicken on this simple sandwich. Pack it in your cooler bag for a post-workout meal at the gym.

**Bacon-Apple Chicken Sandwich Recipe:**

**Ingredients:**
- 2 slices Julian Bakery Coconut Paleo Bread
- 3 slices uncured thick-cut bacon
- 1 oz deli-sliced roasted chicken breast
- 2 tsp Knudson's Organic Apple Butter
- 6 leaves baby spinach

**Directions:** Place the bacon in a heavy pan set over medium heat. When it sizzles and is browning on one side, flip it over with metal tongs and cook on the other side until crisp, about 6 minutes total. Drain on a plate covered with paper towel.

To assemble the sandwich: Spread one teaspoon of apple butter on one side of each slice of bread. On one slice, layer the chicken, then the bacon, then the spinach. Top with the other apple-buttered slice of bread. Enjoy right away, or wrap in waxed paper and pack it in your cooler bag for lunch or a post-workout meal.

* For quicker sandwich making, cook an entire package of bacon and store it in an airtight container in the refrigerator for use throughout the week!

Serving Size: 1 sandwich    Yields: 1 serving
Prep Time: 4 min    Cook Time: (bacon) 6 min    Total Time: 10 min

BANANA
SANDWICH

# SIMPLE BANANA SANDWICH

This sandwich is a favorite for both kids and grown-ups! Perfect for a pre-workout energy boost or as a lunch box lunch, it's full of protein and healthy carbohydrates to keep you running strong. If you don't go through the Julian Bakery Paleo Almond Bread quickly, keep it in your freezer and just pop what you need in the toaster to thaw.

**Simple Banana Sandwich Recipe:**

**Ingredients:**
- 1 small banana
- 2 slices Julian Bakery Paleo Almond Bread
- 1 tbsp organic apple butter
- 1 tbsp natural almond butter

**Directions:** Peel and slice the banana into rounds. Spread one tablespoon of almond butter on one slice of bread. Spread the apple butter on the other slice of bread. Spread the bananas evenly on top of the almond butter. Place the apple butter slice on top of the banana, apple-side-down. Enjoy with a cold glass of almond milk.

Serving Size: 1 sandwich      Yields: 1 serving
Prep Time: 5 minutes      Total Time: 5 minutes

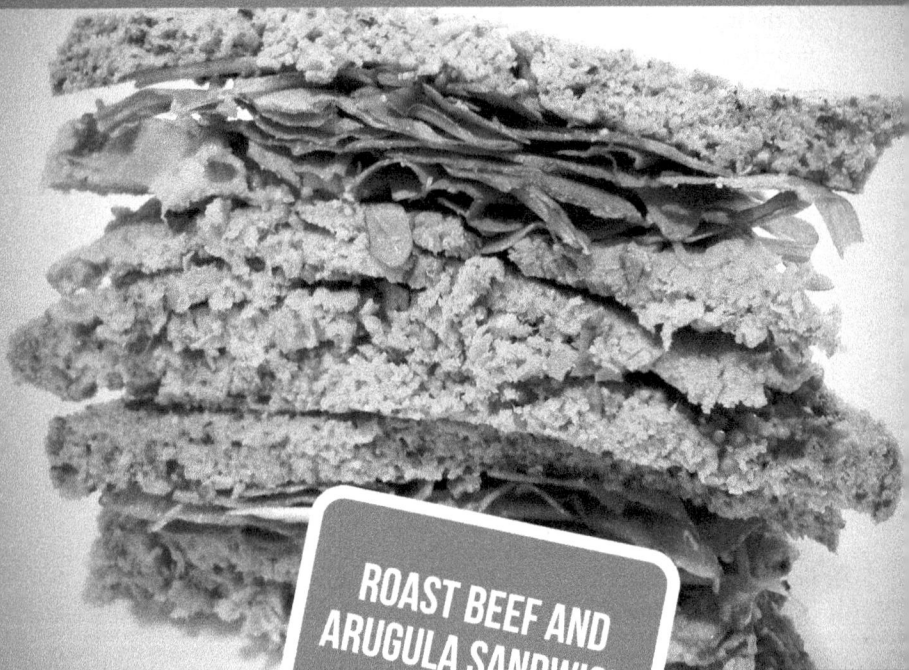

ROAST BEEF AND
ARUGULA SANDWICH

# ROAST BEEF AND ARUGULA SANDWICH

Sandwiches are a lunchtime standard that you may have been missing since you've been eating a Paleo diet. This roast beef sandwich will have you salivating before you're even done making it! You can use deli roast beef, or thinly sliced beef from a leftover roast. With the Julian Bakery Paleo Almond Bread, you'll have the convenience of a sandwich without the process of making grain-free bread!

**Roast Beef And Arugula Sandwich Recipe:**

**Ingredients:**
- 2 slices Julian Bakery Paleo Almond Bread
- 3 slices deli roast beef
- ½ cup baby arugula
- 2 tsp stone ground garlic mustard

**Directions:** Spread one teaspoon mustard on one side of each slice of bread. Layer with roast beef and arugula. Enjoy with sweet potato chips.

Serving Size: 1 sandwich     Yields: 1 serving
Prep Time: 3 min     Total Time: 3 min

NAKED
TUNA WRAP

# NAKED TUNA WRAP

This tuna salad is naked because, well, it's undressed! You really don't miss the mayo in this deliciously simple tuna wrap recipe. Keep the Julian Bakery Paleo wraps on hand. They're essentially dehydrated coconut, so they keep for weeks in the pantry.

**Naked Tuna Wrap Recipe:**

**Ingredients:**
- 2 Julian Bakery Paleo Wraps
- 1 5 oz can chunk or solid white tuna in water
- 1 tbsp minced celery
- 1 tbsp minced green onion
- ½ tsp celery salt
- Ground black pepper to taste

**Directions:** Drain the water from the can of tuna and place fish in a small bowl. Mince the celery and light portions of the green onion. Place them in the bowl with the tuna and add the salt and pepper. Mash well with the back of a fork.

Divide filling evenly between the two wraps, spreading it so it covers the center portion from one end to the other. Roll, slice, and serve.

Serving Size: 1 wrap     Yields: 2 servings
Prep Time: 5 min    Total Time: 5 min

# DINNER

After a long, busy day, the last thing you want to do is start prepping a three-hour meal. With these fool-proof recipes, you'll be at the table in minutes rather than hours. Paleo doesn't have to mean "painstaking!" Simple, prepared ingredients make caveman dinner time a breeze.

# DINNER MENU

**DELECTABLE CHICKEN DRUMSTICKS** (FREEZER / TAKE AWAY)

**ALL-DAY BABY BACK RIBS** (FREEZER / SLOW-COOKER)

**BEEF AND BUTTERNUT STEW** (FREEZER / SLOW-COOKER)

**ANDOUILLE SAUSAGE STIR FRY** (QUICK)

**ITALIAN FRITTATA** (QUICK)

**EGGPLANT FREEZER CASSEROLE** (FREEZER)

**WAFFLE IRON STEAK AND PORTABELLA** (QUICK)

**PUMPKIN CURRY SOUP** (QUICK / FREEZER)

**FIFTEEN-MINUTE CHILI** (QUICK / FREEZER)

**FIESTA SWEET POTATO** (POST-WORKOUT)

DELECTABLE
CHICKEN DRUMSTICKS

# DELECTABLE CHICKEN DRUMSTICKS

These chicken drumsticks are so ridiculously easy and delicious; you'll probably end up making a batch every week. They are fantastic hot right out of the oven, and just as good cold in the lunch box. They also freeze well, so you can pack them up in a glass container with a tight-fitting lid and freeze them until you're ready to use them. Good luck, though, they never last that long in our house!

**Delectable Chicken Drumstick Recipe:**

**Ingredients:**
- 10 free-range, organic chicken legs
- 1 Tbsp garlic powder
- ½ Tbsp sea salt (or to taste)
- 1 tsp smoked paprika
- 1 Tbsp coconut oil

**Directions:** Preheat oven to 375 °F.
In a large bowl, mix together the garlic powder, sea salt, and paprika. Rinse the chicken legs and rub with coconut oil. This will help the skin crisp up as you bake the chicken. Toss the drumsticks in the seasoning and place on a rimmed baking dish.

Bake at 375 °F for 45 – 55 minutes (depending on size of drumsticks) or until a meat thermometer inserted into the largest piece reaches at least 165 °F. Serve immediate with sweet potato fries and cabbage slaw, or store in the refrigerator for up to five days. The chicken can also be frozen and reheated in the oven when needed. Simple remove it from the freezer and place in a single layer on a rimmed pan, and bake at 350 °F for about a half hour.

Tip: You can throw in home cut sweet potato fries in the oven at the same time, then you have a complete meal ready all at once!

Serving Size: 2 drumsticks       Yields: 5 servings
Prep Time: 10 min       Bake Time: 45 min       Total Time: 55 min

ALL-DAY BABY
BACK RIBS

# ALL-DAY BABY BACK RIBS

If you just take a couple of minutes in the morning to prep these ribs, you'll have the most mouth-watering meal when you walk in the door after work or school... or a day at the beach! Pair these with a delicious baked sweet potato and you have a dinner worthy of the best rib joint in town.

**All-Day Baby back Ribs Recipe:**

**Ingredients:**
- 2 slabs baby back pork ribs (as always, grass-fed, organic, hormone-free)
- 4 Tbsp apple cider vinegar
- 2 Tbsp gluten-free Worcestershire sauce
- 2 tsp prepared chopped garlic
- 1 tsp smoked paprika
- 2 Tbsp pure maple syrup

**Directions:** Rinse the ribs and cut to fit into your slow cooker. I generally cut mine into 4-rib sections. Place them in the bottom of your slow cooker, meaty side up. They will be layered, and that's okay.

In a small bowl, whisk together the sauce ingredients. Pour the sauce over the ribs, making sure to coat all the meat. Use up all the sauce, letting it drain to the bottom of the pot when all the meat is coated.

Turn the slow cooker on low for 7 – 9 hours, or high for 4 – 6 hours. When you're ready to serve the ribs, gently lift them out of the pan onto a jelly roll pan with the meaty side up. Baste with the liquid from the bottom of the slow cooker. Broil on low for 4 – 5 minutes for a nice, crisp, caramelized texture. *This step is optional, but delicious if you have time.

Serve with a salad and baked sweet potatoes, or sweet potato fries and cole slaw. You can save the remaining ribs (if you have any left) in an airtight container in the refrigerator or freezer. Simply bake in the oven to reheat, or eat them cold!

Serving Size: ½ rack        Yields: 4 servings        Prep Time: 5 min  Slow
Cook Time: 4 – 9 hours        Total: 4 – 9 hrs + 5 min

BEEF AND
BUTTERNUT STEW

# BEEF AND BUTTERNUT STEW

This stew comes together quickly with pre-cut stew meat and cubed butternut squash from the produce coolers. Get the slow cooker started in the morning before work, and when you get home after a long day, the delicious smells will wrap you in warmth. It will feel like someone cooked you dinner, and don't we all deserve that once in a while?

**Beef And Butternut Stew Recipe:**

**Ingredients:**
- 1 lb grass-fed beef stew meat
- 2 lbs cubed butternut squash
- 1 cup frozen diced onion
- 3 cups organic beef broth
- 1 Tbsp gluten free Worcestershire sauce
- 1 Tbsp tapioca starch
- 1 tsp prepared minced garlic (from a jar)
- 1 whole bay leaf
- Sea salt and black pepper to taste

**Directions:** Place the beef cubes in the bottom of a large slow cooker and sprinkle with the tapioca starch. Turn to coat. Add the remaining ingredients, except broth, and mix well with a spoon or your hands. Pour over the broth to cover the meat and vegetables, adding more if necessary.

Turn slow cooker on low for eight hours, or high for 4 – 5 hours. Serve hot with as is or poured over whipped cauliflower.

This stew also freezes well. Pour into individual lidded glass bowls or a large airtight container. When ready to eat, run water around the container and slide the frozen stew out into the crock pot. Heat several hours until the stew is warmed through.

Serving Size: ¼ recipe    Yields: 4 servings
Prep Time: 10 min    Slow-Cook Time: 4 – 8 hrs

# ANDOUILLE SAUSAGE STIR-FRY

# ANDOUILLE SAUSAGE STIR-FRY

Smoked sausage is a quick protein base for a Paleo dinner because it's already seasoned and only needs to be warmed. Andouille sausage has a nice, spicy kick to it. But for this recipe, you can really use any organic, additive-free fully cooked smoked sausage.

**Andouille Sausage Stir-Fry Recipe:**

**Ingredients:**
- 2 links Andouille (or other) smoked sausage
- 32 oz bag California frozen vegetables (cauliflower, carrots, green beans, onion, peppers) or your favorite blend
- 2 Tbsp coconut oil
- 1 tsp prepared minced garlic
- ½ tsp dried basil
- ½ tsp ground coriander
- ¼ tsp dried tarragon
- Cracked black pepper and sea salt to taste

**Directions:** Slice the sausage diagonally into ½" section pieces.
In a large skillet, heat the coconut oil over medium-high heat. Add the sausage and cook for about three minutes until it gets sizzling. Add the vegetables and spices. Continue to cook for eight to ten minutes, stirring every few minutes, until the vegetables are heated through but not mushy. Serve hot!

Serving Size: ¼ recipe       Yields: 4 servings
Prep Time: 2 min         Cook Time: 10 min         Total Time: 12 min

ITALIAN
FRITTATA

# ITALIAN FRITTATA

This frittata tastes like a fresh margarita pizza, only better! With all the flavors of your favorite Italian foods, but none of the fuss over boiling noodles or cooking meats, this frittata is a great option for a delicious meal in a snap. You can even slice and store it in the refrigerator for quick lunches. It's just as good cold!

**Italian Frittata Recipe:**

**Ingredients:**
- 6 large eggs
- 2 cups packed baby spinach
- 12 grape tomatoes
- 2 tsp minced garlic
- 2 tbsp coconut oil or ghee
- 1 tsp dried oregano
- 1 tsp dried basil
- Salt and black pepper to taste

**Directions:** In a medium bowl, whisk the eggs with 2 tablespoons of water until frothy. Stir in the baby spinach, garlic, oregano, basil, salt and pepper. Halve the tomatoes and set aside.

Heat the oil in the bottom of a cast iron skillet set over low heat. Pour in the egg mixture and cook until the center begins to bubble. Push back the edge of the frittata with a rubber spatula. Tilt the pan to fill in the turned space. Do this two more times on other spots in the pan. This will allow the frittata to cook evenly.

Preheat the broiler to low.

When the eggs look like they are nearly set, with just a slight bit of run on the top, evenly distribute the grape tomatoes. Set the entire skillet under the broiler and broil for about two minutes, or until the top of the eggs is cooked through and the tomatoes are softening.

Slice into triangles and serve with a fresh baby field green salad.

Serving Size: ¼ of frittata     Yields: 4 servings
Prep Time: 5 min     Cook Time: 15 min     Total Time: 20 min

EGGPLANT FREEZER
CASSEROLE

# EGGPLANT FREEZER CASSEROLE

This eggplant casserole is easy to put together and can be frozen until you're in need of a no-work meal! The photo is of casserole before it's been cooked, so this is what it will look like when you put it into the freezer. Double the recipe and make two pans... eat one now and freeze one for later!

**Eggplant Freezer Casserole Recipe:**

**Ingredients:**
- 1 small eggplant
- 1 16 oz can tomato sauce or prepared marinara sauce
- 1 8 oz carton sliced baby bella mushrooms
- ¼ cup pre-diced white onion (fresh or frozen)
- 1 tsp dried basil
- 1 tsp salt

**Directions:** Wash and slice the eggplant into very thin rounds. Rinse the mushrooms. Cover the bottom of a 10" square glass or aluminum baking dish with tomato sauce. Top with a layer of eggplant rounds, overlapping each round slightly. Sprinkle with salt.

Layer ½ of the mushrooms over the eggplant and sprinkle on 1/3 of the onion. Cover in sauce. Repeat these steps until all of the eggplant and sauce have been used. End with a layer of eggplant covered in sauce, onion, and basil.

Cover with a tight-fitting lid and freeze until ready to use, up to two months. When ready to use, preheat oven to 350°F. Remove casserole from the freezer and remove lid. Cover with aluminum foil and bake for 45 minutes covered. Remove foil and bake an additional 45 minutes uncovered or until the eggplant is soft and the sauce is bubbling. Cool on a rack for ten minutes before serving.

To bake from fresh: Bake in the preheated oven for one hour.

*It's important that you use a baking dish that can go straight from freezer to oven. If you don't have such a pan, make sure to allow your casserole to thaw for several hours before baking.

Serving Size: 1 ½ cups        Yields: 4 servings
Prep Time: 10 min        Bake Time From Frozen: 90 minutes

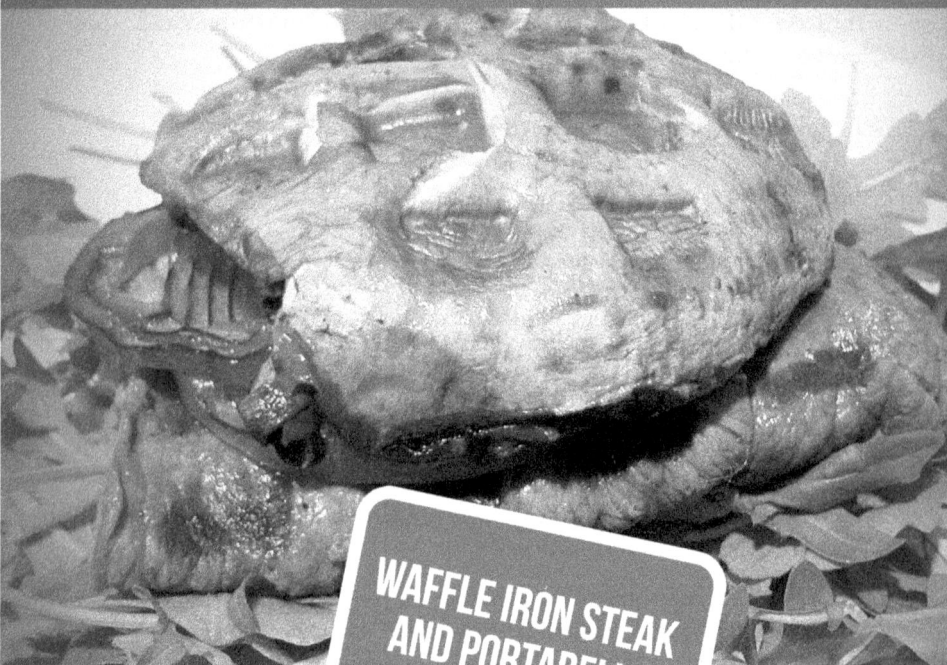

WAFFLE IRON STEAK
AND PORTABELLA

# WAFFLE IRON STEAK AND PORTABELLA

Waffle irons aren't just for breakfast anymore! An electric waffle iron can cook you a meal in just a few minutes with minimal cleanup and perfectly cooked meats and veggies. This thinly sliced top sirloin steak and Portabella mushroom stack is a delicious last-minute meal that will stand up to a gourmet steak any day!

**Waffle Iron Steak And Portabella Recipe:**

**Ingredients:**
- 1 large Portabella mushroom cap, stem removed
- 1 very thin slice red onion
- 1 thin sliced top sirloin steak (or other steak sliced ¼" thick or less)
- Olive oil or olive oil cooking spray for coating
- Salt and ground black pepper
- 1 cup baby arugula for serving

**Directions:** Preheat your double-waffle iron according to manufacturer directions. Rinse the mushroom cap and remove the stem. Season both the steak and mushroom well with salt and fresh cracked black pepper (or seasoning of choice).

Spray the top and bottom of the preheated waffle iron with olive oil to prevent sticking. Lay the steak on one side of the waffle maker, folding it over to fit. Top the steak with the onion slice. Lay the mushroom on the other side of the waffle maker. Close the lid.

The lid may not close all the way, but that's okay. It will settle as the mushroom cooks down. You can press down gently as it cooks.

Cook for about four minutes, or until the mushroom has softened, the steak is medium-well (or to order), and the onion is beginning to caramelize. Serve over a bed of baby arugula.

Serving Size: 1 recipe      Yields: 1 serving
Prep Time: 3 min      Cook Time: 4 min      Total Time: 7 min

PUMPKIN
CURRY SOUP

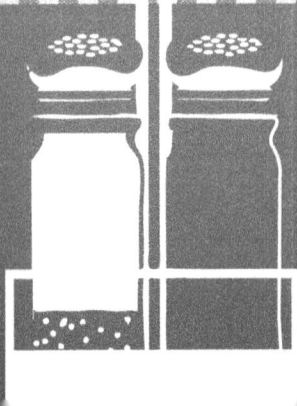

# PUMPKIN CURRY SOUP

A can of organic pureed pumpkin turns into delicious Indian-inspired soup in a matter of minutes with the addition of chicken stock and spices. For extra deliciousness, serve this soup with a dollop of unsweetened coconut whipped cream or add a little plain coconut milk just before serving.

**Pumpkin Curry Soup Recipe:**

**Ingredients:**
- 1 15oz can pureed pumpkin
- 2 cups chicken broth
- 1 ½ tsp curry powder
- ½ tsp coriander
- Sea salt to taste
- 2 Tbsp coconut milk or coconut whipped cream (optional)
- Chives for garnish (optional)

**Directions:** Place the pumpkin puree, chicken broth, curry powder, coriander, and sea salt in a saucepan and set over medium heat. Whisk the ingredients together until smooth. Heat through, stirring occasionally, about five minutes.

Pour into two bowls and garnish with chives and coconut whipped cream (optional).

Serving Size: 2 cups      Yields: 2 servings
Prep Time: 2 min      Cook Time: 5 min      Total Time: 7 min

FIFTEEN-MINUTE
CHILI

# FIFTEEN-MINUTE CHILI

This Mexican-inspired chili is hearty and satisfying, and comes together in just ten minutes! Make a double recipe and freeze leftovers in glass containers. You can heat one up on one of those nights when you're too busy for even ten minutes. This chili tastes just as good, or even better, the second time around.

**Fifteen-Minute Chili Recipe:**

Ingredients:
- 1 lb grass-fed organic ground beef
- 1 28 oz can organic diced tomatoes in juice (not in oil)
- 1 12 oz bag frozen chopped three-pepper and onion medley
- 2 heaping teaspoons taco seasoning (see recipe below)

**Taco Seasoning:**  In a glass jar, mix together 2 Tbsp chili powder, 1 tsp garlic powder, ½ tsp onion powder, ½ tsp dried oregano, 1 tsp smoked paprika, 3 tsp cumin, and 2 tsp sea salt. Store in an airtight jar for up to three months.

**Directions:**  Place ground beef in a large pot and break up the meat with a wooden spoon. Cook over medium heat, stirring regularly, until the meat is starting to brown. Add in the frozen peppers and onion. Continue to cook, stirring occasionally, until the vegetables are tender and the meat is browned. Add the can of diced tomatoes with juices and the taco seasoning. Stir to mix, and heat over medium-high heat until the chili is heated through. Enjoy right away, pack in a thermos for a hearty lunch, or freeze up to a month in sealed glass containers.

Serving Size: 2 cups          Yields:  about 8 servings
Prep Time:  5 min          Cook Time:  8 – 10 min
Total Time: 15 min

FIESTA
SWEET POTATO

# FIESTA SWEET POTATO

After you engage in vigorous physical activity, your body needs to replenish its carbohydrates and protein. Plan ahead by sticking the potato in the oven before you go out for your run or jump on the elliptical. This way it will be piping hot and ready for topping after you get out of the shower.

**Fiesta Sweet Potato Recipe:**

**Ingredients:**
- 1 medium sweet potato (yam)
- ¾ cup leftover 15-MINUTE CHILI  *see recipe on page 65

**Directions:**  Preheat oven to 400°F. Scrub the sweet potato and pierce it several times with a fork. Wrap the potato in foil and bake in the preheated oven for one hour, or until tender.

Go for your workout! When you're done, you can heat up your chili for topping. The great thing about the potato is that its cook time is flexible. You can leave it for up to a half-hour longer and it will be fine.

Reheat your leftover chili in a pot on the stove. Using oven mitts (because the potato will be hot), peel off the foil and cut the potato down the center lengthwise. Press both ends toward the center to split the potato open. Add the chili topping with a slotted spoon (to drain out excess juice).

Serving Size: 1 potato      Yields: 1 serving
Prep Time: 5 minutes      Bake time: 1 hour      Total: 1 hr, 5 min

# AN EASY ALTERNATIVE

Let's face it, our lives can get really busy. We don't always have time to sit down and eat a meal, let alone cook it fresh. That's why there's a huge market for power bars, granola bars, breakfast cookies, and any other handheld food that can nourish our bodies. While you can stock your pantry with LARA bars, these homemade treats are just as delicious and are a fraction of the cost.

# MEAL REPLACEMENTS

### APRICOT ENERGY COOKIE
(PRE-WORKOUT / QUICK / PANTRY STAPLE / TAKE AWAY)

### NOATMEAL RAISIN COOKIE PROTEIN BAR
(PRE-WORKOUT / QUICK / PANTRY STAPLE / TAKE AWAY)

APRICOT ENERGY COOKIE

# APRICOT ENERGY COOKIE

This cookie is the perfect energy boost for a pre-workout fix. Packed with natural sugars from dried fruits, protein, and chia, you can power up your performance or simply eat one as a meal replacement on a day that you're too rushed to cook.

**Apricot Energy Cookie Recipe:**

**Ingredients:**
- 1 cup raw almonds
- ½ cup dried apricots
- ½ cup coconut flour
- 3 pitted Medjool dates
- 2 large eggs
- 3 tbsp coconut oil
- 2 tsp chia seeds
- ¼ tsp baking soda
- ½ tsp Allspice

**Directions:** Preheat oven to 350°F.
Place the almonds, apricots, dates, and flour into your food process and chop until a mealy dough forms. Add the eggs, coconut oil, baking soda, and Allspice. Pulse until an even, soft dough forms.

Scoop by the ¼ cup-full onto a lightly greased baking sheet. Bake in the preheated oven for ten minutes, or until the cookies are set. Cool on a wire rack. Store in an airtight container in the cupboard for up to ten days.

Serving Size: 1 cookie    Yields: 5 servings
Prep Time: 5 min    Bake Time: 10 min    Total Time: 15 min

NOATMEAL
RAISIN BAR

# NOATMEAL RAISIN COOKIE PROTEIN BAR

This bar is similar to LARA Bars and only takes a few minutes to throw together. One batch will provide you with a week's worth of breakfasts on the fly, or pre-workout fuel that's easy to throw into your gym bag. They are shelf-stable for up to two weeks, or can be frozen for up to a couple of months. The flavor is so much like an oatmeal cookie that you'll feel like you're treating yourself to dessert.

**Noatmeal Raisin Cookie Protein Bar Recipe:**

**Ingredients:**
- 1 cup raw almonds
- ½ cup pitted Medjool dates
- ½ cup raisins
- 1 ½ tsp cinnamon
- 1 tsp vanilla

**Directions:** Place all ingredients into the food processor and process until a "dough ball" forms, about three minutes. Remove to a sheet of waxed paper. Place another sheet of waxed paper on top of the dough and roll out with a pastry roller.

Shape into a 12" rectangle. Remove the top sheet of waxed paper and slice into six "bars." Wrap the bars in waxed paper and store in an airtight container in the cupboard for up to three weeks or more. These travel well and are perfect for a pre-workout boost!

Serving Size: 1 bar          Yields: 6 servings
Prep Time: 10 min          Total Time: 10 min

SWEET POTATO
FRIES

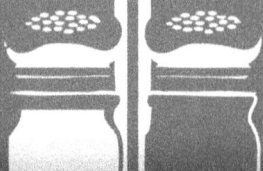

BONUS RECIPE!

# SWEET POTATO FRIES
## ( BONUS RECIPE FROM 'THE PALEO KID' )

Okay, I'll let you in on a dirty little secret... My kids and I are french fry junkies. We love them with chicken, or burgers, or by themselves dunked in catsup or honey mustard. On the paleo diet, we try to limit our intake of white potatoes. Even though they are technically allowed, they are kind of empty calories. But we can still get our fry fix by substituting nutrient-rich sweet potatoes for the starchy white tubers.

**Sweet Potato Fries Recipe:**

**Ingredients:**
- 2 large sweet potatoes
- 1 quart coconut oil (or: lard / duck fat / tallow)

**Directions:** In a medium heavy pot, or a deep fryer, heat the oil until it's very hot, about ten minutes. While it's heating, peel the sweet potato and remove bad spots. Slice into desired shapes with a very sharp knife. (Or if you have pre-cut and pre-frozen the sweet potato strips, skip the peeling and slicing steps.)

Carefully drop the fries into the hot oil. Be careful, the oil may splatter or pop. Fry until the fries are golden and crisp. The time can vary based on the size of cut, the heat of the oil, and the size of the pan. Just watch them carefully. It should take 5 to 7 minutes.

With a slatted spoon, remove fries to a plate covered with paper towel. Shake on sea salt to taste. Let cool for a few minutes before serving.

**TO MAKE SWEET POTATO CHIPS:** Use the same recipe, but instead of cutting into fry shapes, use a mandolin or very sharp knife to slice the potatoes paper thin. Fry in the oil for about 2 – 4 minutes.

These fries can be frozen and heated in the oven later. Simply spread them out on a parchment lined baking pan and freeze until they're frozen through. Then empty them into a zip-top bag. When ready to use, bake them in a 350° oven for about 15 minutes or until heated through and crisp.

*You can save the oil in a mason jar to use again for your next batch of fries!

Serving size: ½ potato          Yields: 2 servings
Prep time: 5 min          Cook time: 7 min          Total time: 12 min

# ABOUT THE AUTHOR

**Kate Evans Scott** is the author of the Amazon Bestselling cookbooks The Paleo Kid, Paleo Kid Snacks, The Paleo Kid Lunchbox, The Paleo Kid's Halloween, The Paleo Kid's Christmas and Infused: 26 Spa-Inspired Vitamin Waters. After her son was diagnosed with several food intolerances and after having struggled with her own Autoimmune Disease, Kate made the commitment to remove all grains and processed foods from her family's diet. Her passion and love for good food blossomed after training with a retreat chef in Belgium in her early 20's. Since then, she has wanted to bring her love of food and health into the kitchens of other families struggling with health and dietary challenges.

Kate creates delicious dishes that are suitable for those suffering from digestive and autoimmune diseases - meals that nourish the body while healing the gut. Kate and her husband Mark live in Oregon with their two spirited children.

# MORE BY KATE EVANS SCOTT

Available Now on Amazon

Available Now on Amazon

Available Now on Amazon

Available Now on Amazon

Available Now on Amazon

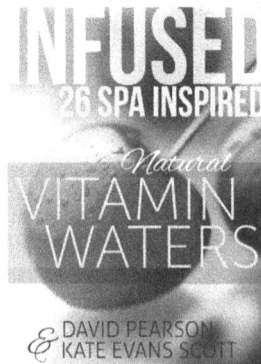

Available Now on Amazon

# RECIPE NOTES

# RECIPE NOTES

# RECIPE NOTES

www.ingramcontent.com/pod-product-compliance
Lightning Source LLC
Chambersburg PA
CBHW071455070426
42452CB00040B/1530